Richard Branson Failure and Success

The history of a Billionaire

Table of Contents

Copyright

Introduction

I want to thank you and congratulate you for downloading the book, *Richard Branson Failure and Success: The History of a Billionaire.*

This book contains the life story of Richard Branson, the world-famous founder of the Virgin Group of Companies.

In this book, you will see how Richard Branson struggled through life as a kid and how he experienced failures but didn't let it faze him. His story is something anyone can learn life lessons from. Reading about him can awaken inspiration in anyone.

Thanks again for downloading this book, I hope you enjoy it!

Chapter 1: Who is Richard Branson?

"Don't be embarrassed by your failures. Learn from them and start again." – Richard Branson

The most inspiring success stories are not about people having everything fall in the right place. They are not about people who get everything done correctly the first time. They are not about a smooth sailing ride towards the top.

The most inspiring success stories are actually about people who experienced failure. They fall down, get mocked and discouraged by others, and even hated by some. The roads they had to take towards success were rough – full of bumps and obstacles. The greatness comes not because they didn't experience hardships, but because they did and came out triumphant in the end.

Such is the story of Richard Branson. In his early life, Richard Branson went through tough times especially with his academic endeavors. The people around him likely couldn't or didn't imagine him as the billionaire he is today. His story is one that can teach many life lessons to anyone.

His full name is Sir Richard Charles Nicholas Branson. He was born on July 18, 1950 in Blackheath, London. He is the eldest child of James Branson, a barrister, and Eve Huntley Branson, a flight attendant. His grandfather, Right Honourable Sir

George Arthur Harwin Branson, was Privy Councillor and a judge at the High Court of Justice at the time.

Richard Branson is an investor and business magnate perhaps most popular for founding the Virgin Group composed of more than 400 companies.

His Academic Struggle

When Richard Branson was a child, the academic world is his main challenge. He went to Scaitcliffe School, an all-boys school which is now renamed to Bishopgate School, until the age of thirteen. He then transferred to Stowe School, a boarding school located in Stowe, Buckinghamshire, England, until the age of sixteen. More discussions later about what he did after this.

He struggled because he was born with dyslexia, a condition labeled as a learning disability. His academic performance suffered because of this almost failing Scaitcliffe. The struggle continued in Stowe. At the age of sixteen, he dropped out of school.

Dropping Out of School

After dropping out of school, Richard Branson started his career. From the crypt of a church, he began a youth-culture magazine titled *Student*. The magazine was meant for students and students also run it. It launched in the year 1966, selling $8,000 worth of advertising in its first edition. The *Student*'s first run, consisting of 50,000 copies, were distributed for free. Branson covered the costs with the advertising.

By the year 1969, Branson was residing in a London commune. All around him is the British music and drug scene. It was at this time that Branson came up with an idea for funding the costs of his publication. This is in the form of a mail-order record company that he traded under the name *Virgin*.

Virgin experienced modest earnings in the beginning but it was enough to motivate Branson to push his efforts. Branson didn't plan to stay that way. So, from the modest performance, he began to expand his business ventures.

Awards and Recognition

"And you know, I've had great fun turning quite a lot of different industries on their head and making sure those industries will never be the same again, because Virgin went in and took them on." – Richard Branson

Richard Branson has definitely made a name for himself. While he did received criticism and even derogatory labels along the way, there are people who recognized his achievements. The changes he pioneered did not go unappreciated.

Branson belongs to the famous and successful drop-outs. He dropped out of school since he realized the academe is not tolerable of a dyslexic like him. But, in 1993, Loughborough University recognized his intellect. They gave Branson an honorary degree of Doctor of Technology.

Elizabeth II believed in Branson's contributions, particularly, his "services to entrepreneurship". In the New Year's Honours list of December 30 1999, she signified her intention to present the honour of Knight Bachelor to Branson.

In March of 2000, Charles, Prince of Wales knighted Richard Branson in Buckingham Palace at an investiture.

His ventures in the airline business were also commendable and it's hard to deny his accomplishments. Branson received the Tony Jannus Award for them also in the year 2000.

Branson acts as a patron for several charities, including the International Rescue Corps and Prisoners Abroad.

Branson secured the no. 85 spot on the 2002 list of 100 Great Britons – a list sponsored by BBC and voted for by the public. The world-renowned Time Magazine also included Richard Branson in its 2007 Top 100 Most Influential People in the World.

December of 2007, Branson received the United Nations Correspondents Association Citizen of the World Award from UN Secretary General Ban Ki-Moon due to his aid for the humanitarian and environmental causes.

On January of 2011, Branson joined the ranks of Bill Clinton and the Dalai Lama when he was awarded with the German Media Prize.

Richard Branson's Properties

In addition to his wealth and business ventures, Richard Branson is also well-known for his tangible properties found in various parts of the world.

The Private Game Reserve and Lodge

Located in South Africa, this is a 13,500-hectare area of untouched African bush where travelers can roam in search for the Big Five. The Private Game Reserve is situated in the Sabi Sand Reserve at the border of Kruger National Park. The reserve offers you an utmost luxurious place to stay since they offer two very different lodges that you can choose from.

The first lodge that you will find in the Private Game Reserve is the Rock Lodge. It is situated on the summit of a rocky hill. You can find panoramic views of the jungle where wildlife roams in the area. It has 21 luxury suites with state-of the-art facilities.

The second lodge is the world class accommodation, the Safari Lodge. It is built along the banks of the Mabrak riverbed, with 21 rooms in tree house style so that guests can get the feel of the jungle safari. In your room, you will be able to see the animals strolling going to the watering hole.

The Kasbah Tamadot

Brandon's Kasbah Tamadot is a magical hotel situated at the foothills of the Atlas Mountains. He bought the area in 1998. This hotel features different luxurious suites and provides the feeling of staying in a private home with its friendly staff from the local villages of Berber.

It has 27 spectacular bedroom and suites that includes 9 luxury Berber tents, providing a comfortable place to stay. Each bedroom has a distinct Berber name and is decorated with traditional Moroccan furniture, marvelous artifacts and antiques from all over the world. Other suites have private plunge pools.

The hotel has a striking Kanoun Restaurant, which features a romantic fireside bar and serves delicious international and local flavor cuisines. It also has an indoor/outdoor infinity pool, a tennis court, marvelous fragrant gardens and a well equipped gym.

The Roof Gardens

The Roof Gardens is a unique place in central London. It was built in 1938. It includes themed gardens with more than 70 full size trees, fountains spread across 1 ½ acres, flamingos and a club house. The Roof Garden is 100 feet above Kensington High Street. It is considered as one of the most stylish venues in London. It comprises 3 themed gardens and a club house. It serves as host to several spectacular events such as business meetings, discos, weddings and dinners. The first garden is the English Woodland with mature trees and a lake dwelled by four resident flamingos – Pecks, Bill, Ben and Splosh, and some ducks. Next is the Tudor Garden with evergreen shrubs surrounded by aromatic flowers such as roses, lilies and a fountain. The 3rd one is the Spanish Garden with palm trees offering a unique Moorish flavor. These three gardens can cater to several events for a maximum of 120 guests.

For ease of service, the private members club has several VIP areas and two bars. The club offers a very relaxing atmosphere with attractive charisma and with over 100 talented professionals. The Babylon is an exclusive restaurant that offers attention grabbing décor and sumptuous cuisines to enhance the great experience.

The Lodge Verbier

Richard Branson also owns this pricey asset. This lodge is a division of his Virgin Limited Edition with outstanding design architecture. Complete with great Master suites and several recreational amenities, this lodge provides the best accommodation and pleasure experience. It is situated in Verbier, Switzerland.

This lodge offers state of the art lodging facilities with its two great Master suites and 7 brilliantly adorned luxury bedrooms, where you can view the valley. Each suite has egg-shaped bath with chic rubber ducks. The best site for delicious Swiss and international cuisines is its open plan kitchen. The wine cellar includes an extensive selection of wines. With the lodge's outdoor and indoor Jacuzzis, the level of relaxation is sublime. Each lodge has a living room, a party area with karaoke machine, latest games consoles, DVDs, a well-equipped gym and pool tables.

The Mahali Mzuri

Mahali Mzuri is located in Kenya. This is one of the many Branson's collection of exclusive and eclectic retreats. The luxury Kenyan Safari camp name means beautiful place. This camp is situated in the Motorogi Conservancy in Kenya. It features 12 sleeper tents installed on an elevated platform, with a capacity of 24 guests. Among the 12 sleeper tented suites, 10 of it can be configured with twin bed house two adults while the other two suites have two extra pull down beds for family accommodation. Each suite has a spacious bedroom with an integral bathroom. The tent includes a terrace and a sitting area where you can see the views over the landscape. It has an infinity pool and spa treatment to provide an effective relaxation.

Richard Branson's Necker Belle Yacht

The unique thing about Branson's yacht is that it is one of the few luxury catamarans in the world. It was launched originally as the Lady Barbaretta in 2003. The yacht spent 2 years at Australia's Azzura Marine for refitting. It has a 14 meter beam speed that encompasses 4 en suite stateroom, all above waterline with great views. The yacht interior is very similar to Branson's Necker island retreat and the main cabin's lounge area, which can be transformed into a double cabin.

Chapter 2: Branson Enters the Record Industry

"There is no point in starting your own business unless you do it out of a sense of frustration." – Richard Branson

Richard Branson began his efforts in the business world through the record business. He was not afraid to admit that frustration was what made him start *Virgin*. He sold records with prices that are significantly lower than record shops known as "High Street", most prominently W.H Smith. He named his company *Virgin* following a suggestion of one of his early employees. The suggestion came from the thought that they were all new to business.

Branson's business efforts would later bring about significant innovations which probably no one had foreseen. During that time, many products are priced under limiting marketing agreements. These made strong restrictions on discounting products even in the presence of movement in the 1950s and 1960s for limiting the so-called resale price maintenance. It is here that Branson braved the path of pushing for changes that eventually resulted in an all-encompassing discounting of recorded music.

Later on, Branson was able to start a record shop located in Oxford Street in London. It wasn't long before he faced trouble. In the year 1971, authorities questioned Branson about him selling records that are labeled export stock in the *Virgin* stores. The issue didn't get to a court trial. The agreement ended with Branson repaying any unpaid taxes plus a fine. This resulted in Branson's mother, Eve, having to re-mortgage their family home in order to assist him with the settlement.

Standing Up from a Bad Hit

"You don't learn to walk by following rules. You learn by doing, and by falling over." – Richard Branson

From the bad hit he took, Branson continued his efforts with more fervor. With the earnings from his record store, Branson partnered up with Nik Powell in 1972 and launched the record label *Virgin Records*. They purchased a country estate which they installed with a recording studio.

He opened the recording studio for rent for novice artists without fear. One of the firsts to lease his studio is Mike Oldfield. Assisted by Branson's team, Oldfield recorded his first single *Tubular Bells*. In 1973, Oldfield's first album with the same title became the first release of Virgin Records.

The song *Tubular Bells* was a big hit. It graced the UK charts for a period of 247 weeks. This created a crucial momentum for Virgin Records.

Another artist introduced by Virgin Records that took the world by storm was Culture Club. The band went on to receive prestigious awards and achieve chart-topping hits throughout their career.

Branson proved to have an adventurous spirit as he took risks that others won't. Aside from signing up novices, he also entertained controversial artists – the primary example being the Sex Pistols. Other companies were reluctant to sign them up. What they saw as something to fear, Branson saw as opportunity and he was not wrong. Sex Pistols came out to be one of the most influential bands in the UK.

Another show of bravery that garnered praise for Virgin Records is signing up artists who perform obscure avant-garde music and allowing them to be heard by a larger audience. Faust and Can are some of the artists in this category.

Later on, Branson sold the Virgin label to EMI for £500 million due to his other business ventures. It brought tears to his eyes to let go of the record business as it has been the seed from which the Virgin Empire sprouted. His love for the music business would later be recognized as he created V2 Records just to re-enter.

Aside from Virgin records, Branson expanded his trade mark and established 50 other companies ranging from film-making to hotels, retail, real estate and air conditioner cleaners. In 1983, his sales record reached over 17 million dollars but this feat did not satisfy Branson. He did not stop there. A year later, he ventured into the airline industry and created another company under his famous brand "Virgin Atlantic Airways". This proved to be one of the most precarious undertakings Branson has ever set his mind to for at that time, he was competing against the biggest player in the industry which happened to be British Airways.

Such an undertaking was too big for Branson to handle. Things started to become difficult for Branson and Virgin Atlantic Airways. Fuel prices started to go up beyond what they can afford. Terrorist attacks and threats caused people to fear flying. In addition, British Airways was furtively putting them out of business. This left Branson without any choice but to sell Virgin Records that started his Virgin Empire. He sold it for 1 billion dollars to Thorn-EMI and he used the money to buy back Virgin Atlantic Airways which was then co-owned by the bank. His sacrifice proved to be fruitful since Virgin Atlantic Airways became the second largest international airline in all of Britain.

Branson learned that to achieve something great, he has to sacrifice something of great significance as well. The loss of Virgin Records was simply one of the most devastating blows he had to endure throughout his career. It certainly wasn't easy to give up Virgin Records because it was the foundation of his Virgin Empire. It is what started it all. But he had to sell it in order to save Virgin Atlantic Airways.

The approach "branded venture capital" has become a benchmark of Branson in his business dealings. Before he gained control over other businesses he will first start with licensing his brand name and it was very effective. Currently, Branson is involved in more than 250 companies. He is planning to explore a virgin territory in space by launching his brand name and creating a space shuttle service.

Indeed, be it a personal or a business activity, Branson's determination and passion drove him to achieve what he aims to achieve and break into the unbeaten territory. His courage and deep insights made him who he is today – a businessman worthy of emulation and an inspiration. He is one of the most talked about icons in the business industry not just for his exemplary accomplishments but because he is also one of the most bankable in today's world.

Relevance of Virgin's History to New Entrepreneurs

All things of great importance spring from small ones. The history of Branson's Virgin Empire clearly shows that inexperience or the lack thereof is not to be treated as a hindrance but an asset. Venturing out into the unknown requires tremendous imagination and visualization skills coupled with courage and determination. These are important ingredients to a successful business venture. New and inventive ideas deserved to be discussed with prospective investors and clients for among these ideas, something great might develop. Don't be afraid to tread on unbeaten territories. Face your competitors head on even if they are the sharks in the industry. Play the game fair and square and take the risk. Sacrifice if you must for without sacrifice, there will be nothing to gain.

Whenever you plan on opening up a business, inexperience always makes it possible for you to come up with methods on how you can achieve things differently with unique approach and thinking. Being new in the industry presents good opportunities for you to promote your products and generate publicity and with enthusiasm you can exhaust original ideas and experiment on things that are unfamiliar...in short you can innovate. If you are new, there are so many things to learn. This is a unique advantage that only you can enjoy for established businesses are restricted somehow by past experiences thus, they are not as ready and prepared to venture into the unknown. They just don't have that freedom but you do, so use it to your advantage.

How to avoid common Start-up Mistakes for new entrepreneurs

When starting-up on a business, there are many factors that you need to consider. First, you have to know your product really well. Here are some important questions you need to answer confidently before launching the product or enterprise.

a. What are the selling points of your products?
b. What makes it different from all the other products in the market?
c. What benefits can it give to the customers or consumers in general?
d. Is it affordable by the majority of the masses?
e. What kind of approach will you use that will make you different from the rest?
f. Who are your target markets?
g. How will you reach out to your target markets?
h. Why should consumers choose your services and products over your competitors?

After you honestly answered the following questions, think of a new or different method of presenting your product to the people to get their attention. It is very necessary as most consumers no longer take notice of new products in the market as there are already established brands they can always turn to. Consumers have become wiser now. They value quality over price and quantity. Established brands have established quality so think of the ways on how you can compete with them. Find out what they're lacking and work on that. People will definitely notice your product or service in no time.

Furthermore, before you start-up on an enterprise, look closely into the industry. Is there something new you can add? Is there something lacking that you can fill in? How can you improve customer's experience and satisfaction? With these in mind, you are surely prepared to take on the challenge. Expect that there will be failures along the way. It's normal and failures will give you lessons you can use to improve your products and services. Virgin Empire experienced failures in one way or another. Branson did not stop from there. He moved on and ventured into more unknown territories. He perfected his approach and strengthened hi brand name. Once established, he will venture out again into a different path and try his hard-earned approach and cycle goes on and on.

When Branson experienced his first struggle with his Magazine, they were left with nothing but a small capital. They looked for an empty space in one of the streets in London and they found an old shoe shop. After they were able to talk to the owner to let them use the space, they proceeded with creating a trendy space for the young people who share their passion for music. They do not possess skills in retail but their love for music and enthusiasm prevailed.

Finally, they designed their studio differently. Most studios during their time contain all kinds of music merchandise such as record racks and albums. Branson did not do the same. Instead, they placed large cushions where customers can sit comfortably and built listening booths that gave the place a friendly and enjoyable ambiance.

This different approach made their store really popular and soon they were able to accumulate profits to open up another store until it progressed to be one of the largest music recording industries during their time. Never forget your formula when you first started. Stick by it and apply it whenever necessary. When it worked the first, there is no reason for it not to work the second time. Just add a little different touch and you'll succeed. That is certainly a winning formula you ought to perfect.

Chapter 3: Being an Entrepreneur

"My philosophy is that if I have any money, I invest it in new ventures and not have it sitting around." – Richard Branson

Richard Branson started out with publishing and to support his magazine, he went into selling records. As you have seen in the previous chapter, he climbed his way up in the record industry – seeing opportunity in others' reluctance and pioneering changes throughout the whole industry.

Branson definitely made a name in the record industry, allowing artists to make their own names and leave amazing legacies. Such achievements are fulfilling by themselves. But even better is that they are accompanied with profit. Branson earned a lot, to say the least.

Moving On Out

Branson didn't stop. He delved more into entrepreneurship. Retaining the *Virgin* trade name, he proceeded moving out into other industries.

His ventures into different industries started in 1984 with the establishment of Virgin Atlantic Airways. In the year 1999, he launched Virgin Mobile – a wireless telecommunications subsidiary company. In 2000, he went further still by moving outside the UK and opened Virgin Blue in Australia (now called Virgin Australia).

Why airlines? They are absolutely more than a bit far from publication or music records. Branson has this to say as to what was behind that decision:

"My interest in life comes from setting myself huge, apparently unachievable challenges and trying to rise above them ... from the perspective of wanting to live life to the full, I felt that I had to attempt it."

Branson takes the ways he ran his record company and applies the same principle with his life in general, especially his entrepreneurial endeavors. His brave undertakings just won't stop.

In 1993, Branson once again displayed risk-taking moves by venturing into the railway business. Branson was able to grab the franchises for the Cross-Country sectors of British Rail and the line formerly known as Intercity West Coast. With this, Virgin Trains was born.

Continuing the conquest of the airline scene, the Virgin group of companies obtained the European short-haul airline called Euro Belgian Airlines in 1996. The airline was then renamed into Virgin Express. This airline merged with SN Brussels Airlines in 2006 which formed Brussels Airlines.

Branson's Virgin group of companies relentlessly moved out. Virgin Nigeria, a national airline with Nigeria as its base, was launched. Yet another airline began flights from the San Francisco International Airport in 2007 – Virgin America.

Trials Again...

The continuous expansion of Branson's Virgin group seems to be all ups, but there are also downs. Branson went into development of brands of drinks – the Virgin Cola and Virgin Vodka. They were unsuccessful. The products' mediocre results led into critical responses not only to the products but to Branson and his companies as a whole, most prominently from the British satire magazine Private Eye.

In the early 1990s, a series of disputes arose here and there causing tension between Virgin Atlantic and British Airways. The latter saw the former as an emerging competitor. Virgin repeatedly filed accusations against British Airways as it uses underhanded means to create a bad reputation for Virgin. This ended in British Airways settling the case: they paid Branson £500,000, plus an additional £110,000 to the airline, and legal fees amounting to £3 Million. Branson divided the compensation he got among his staff.

Relentless Expansion

Branson went on towards a lot more business ventures in different industries, including fuel, health, tourism, and entertainment. The Virgin group continued to expand without any signs of stopping.

Branson was dubbed as a "transformational leader" in the lexicon of business management. This is due to his nonconformist strategies and his adamant stand on the Virgin group to be an organization propelled by informality and information – no pressure from a top-level management but rather a bottom-heavy structure.

Charm: Branson's Greatest Asset

Aside from having great determination and self-confidence, another vital key that led to Branson's entrepreneurial success was his charm.

When he was still a neophyte in the field of business, things were quite challenging for him. As a person suffering from dyslexia, understanding business jargons such as 'gross revenue' or 'turnover' was quite a daunting task. He would attend board meetings without any knowledge or clear understanding about the various profit figures that were discussed by his fellow associates.

However, there was something about Richard Branson that made other people respect him. Because of his innate charm, people were willing to help him out and teach him the business jargons that he needed to learn. Without his affable personality and exemplary interpersonal skills, he would not be able to stay as the head of Virgin Group, and manage his empire for so long.

He may not have exemplary mathematical skills, but he knows how to work his way through a successful negotiation. When it comes to closing business deals, he uses the following techniques:

- **Being nice to your negotiators** – By combining Branson's powers of persuasion and his genuinely charming nature, he was able to create successful deals with the most stubborn and hardened negotiators.

- **Never accepting 'no' for a response** – Words such as 'no' or even 'impossible' was never included in Branson's dictionary of business terms. He will always find a way to solve a problem and make sure that he will get the most favorable results.

- **Seek useful professional advice** – The genius entrepreneur understands that there are some things that he just cannot do on his own. That is the reason why he employed a team of advisers who can give him adequate pieces of advice on his professional career. Thanks to these people, he was able to steer his career towards the right path.

Branson's Tips for Starting your Own Business

Unlike most people who inherit their family business, the Virgin Group did not easily fall into Branson's lap. It took him a series successes and failures in order to mold the company into what it is today. Now if you wanted to start your very own business and turn into multi-billion corporation, these are just some of the lessons that you might learn from Richard Branson's success story.

The first lesson that you should remember is to step up and challenge the norm. Always try to break free from the status quo and motivate your team to think outside of the box.

Just take a look at the way Branson refurbished his Virgin Money bank in Britain. Usually, banks follow a standard interior design that is composed of a long line of tellers and windows. In order to improve the customer experience, Branson made sure that every branch of Virgin Money has all the creature comforts that their clients need.

There are a bevy of tables, cozy chairs, reading materials, television sets, and Wi-Fi hotspots to keep their customers relaxed and comfortable while waiting for their turn.

Virgin America Terminal 2, on the other hand, is an airport terminal that is equipped with yoga rooms, a large buffet of delicious food choices, and even art collections.

Another important piece of advice that Branson frequently shares to neophyte entrepreneurs is that they should create a business that will help improve their customer's lives. Before, he was not satisfied with the service that he received from British Airways, so he decided to create Virgin Atlantic – a well-constructed airline that focuses on satisfying the customer's needs and wants.

It is also vital that you have a burning passion for the things that you are doing. If Richard Branson was not enthusiastic in creating a customer-friendly airline, he would not have the drive to exert some effort in looking for a reputable staff, purchasing the aircraft, or making this business become more successful.

In order to make your business pitch successful, you need to make it simple, easy to understand, yet totally memorable. Remove the phrases "we hope that..." in your dictionary. Always be firm and confident when pitching your plans.

Make sure that the plans are concise so that the investors will have an easier time digesting the information. Branson advised that one should avoid presentations with too many numerical figures and complex business theories.

In addition, aspiring entrepreneurs must be able to provide concrete pieces of evidence to prove that their business endeavor is highly sustainable for a long period of time and that it can adapt with the upcoming technological shifts. At a very early age, you must understand that change is inevitable. So you need to create solid plans on how you can help your company survive the sudden technological shifts that will happen in the future.

If you want your startup to be successful in the future, Branson reminds the novice entrepreneurs that they should be exemplary self-motivators. You need to search for the things that will motivate you, and you have to exert a lot of effort in achieving those goals. He also advised that you should never use money as your primary motivator because it will limit the things that you can achieve as a businessman. Just focus on building a company that you will be proud of and money will find its way to your bank account.

Avoiding Startup Pitfalls

As mentioned earlier, Richard Branson's road to success is a very rough one that is filed with a lot of hits and misses. But thanks to these past experiences, he gained more knowledge on how to run a successful business empire. If you want to have a smooth experience when starting your own enterprise, these are the common mistakes that you should definitely avoid.

- **Losing focus** – According to Branson, one should just focus on the present objectives and avoid planning too far ahead. Always keep your business pitch simple and concise. If you keep your pitch nice and short, you will be able to make it clearer, more understandable, and most of all, easier to achieve.

- **Not being realistic with costs** – When it comes to launching your own company, be realistic and expect that you need a lot of money to start one. The JetBlue, for instance, needed $160 million in order for it to be built. Common wisdom states that this cost is too large and it is impossible to raise that kind of money. However, Branson proved them all wrong and they managed to launch JetBlue. Moreover, they were able to gain profit in just six months since the airline's inception.

- **Hiring people just because you like them** – Most people would rather surround themselves with colleagues that they like rather than people who have exceptional skills. Branson advised that as much as possible, do not work with your circle of friends. If the time comes that your team is not performing well and you have to let someone go, doing that might be a very devastating thing to do.

- **Not knowing when to quit** – Good entrepreneurs know when it is time to say goodbye to their CEO positions. You must understand that you are doing this not because you are completely giving up on the business, but because you need to channel more of your energy on another important role.

Importance of fun at work

Being a successful entrepreneur does not mean that you need to overwork. Not only is it harmful to your health, but it can also negatively affect your overall work performance. Richard Branson advised that entrepreneurs should also take some time off from work and enjoy the company of their family or friends. This will help you become more relaxed and have renewed energy to face the upcoming challenges that your company will face.

In addition, another important lesson that Branson wants you to remember is that you should not take failure too seriously. Never forget to smile because a positive attitude will surely motivate you to get back on your feet after you committed a huge mistake.

Chapter 4: Looking Towards the Future

"For a successful entrepreneur it can mean extreme wealth. But with extreme wealth comes extreme responsibility. And the responsibility for me is to invest in creating new businesses, create jobs, employ people, and to put money aside to tackle issues where we can make a difference." – Richard Branson

Richard Branson loves to look toward the future. He is a strong believer of the importance of preparing one's mind for any possibility and keeping a positive outlook in life. As such, Branson invests strongly on technologies and other innovations that he feels have the potential to make a difference for the future of mankind.

Realization: Global Warming

Branson opened up Virgin Fuels which is meant to address global warming and deal with the ever increasing fuel costs by presenting an innovative low-cost fuel for use in automobiles and, eventually, aircraft. Prior to this, Branson was a skeptic about global warming. He stated later that his change of mind was influenced by a breakfast meeting with American politician Al Gore.

In the month of September of the year 2006, Branson made an oath to invest the profits gained from Virgin Atlantic and

Virgin Trains into researching environment-friendly fuel. The estimated amount of this investment is $3 billion.

Healthcare

Branson also saw potential on stem cell treatment. In February of 2007, he launched the Virgin Health Bank. This is for soon-to-be parents to have an opportunity to keep their child's stem cells taken from umbilical cord blood into public and private stem cell banks.

Yet another display of Branson's open-minded ventures happened in 2008. Branson announced that Virgin Healthcare would open a number of clinics that would offer homoeopathic and complementary therapies in addition to conventional medical care. It garnered a positive feedback from that time's UK health minister Ben Bradshaw.

Virgin Earth Challenge

In 2007, Branson announced the establishment of a new global-scale prize for science and technology. It was called the Virgin Earth Challenge. Its main objective is for the good of mankind. Branson believed, according to history, that awards like this drive technological advancements. The Virgin Earth Challenge would reward $25 million to the person or group who can come up and demonstrate a design that is commercially viable meant for the removal of anthropogenic, atmospheric greenhouse gases every year without harmful effects. Further criteria are that the removal technology has to have long-term effects and provide material contribution in stabilizing earth's climate.

Taking People to Space

Innovation in tourism is another aspect that Branson gives a strong outlook into, particularly space tourism. In September of the year 2004, he announced a deal signing for a new company dedicated to the development of space tourism – Virgin Galactic. Virgin Galactic will license the technology that would enable the Spaceship One, a spacecraft that will take people into suborbital space. The development of Spaceship One was funded by co-founder of Microsoft Paul Allen with designs coming from the legendary Burt Rutan, an American aeronautical engineer and visionary. The idea is to take people who are willing to pay into suborbital space as a form of tourist attraction. This plan was featured in one episode of the Discovery channel program *Nextworld*.

What Drives Him to Look Towards the Future

In business circles, Richard Branson is considered as one of the legendary and iconic figures. In fact, his companies span the entire globe. On the other hand, his great desire for a sense of adventure and for brand domination led him to take lots of thought provoking and intriguing risks in the past. His high risk techniques require pushing up to the boundaries as much as possible. All these mixed with a strong sense of foresight and hard work managed to help him make it big in the industry.

Richard Branson believes that to be successful in your endeavor, you have to make sure that your behavior aligns well with what you want to achieve in the long run.

There are numerous subtle and some apparent behaviors that he considers as part of his habit. These enabled him to have greater clarity for his thoughts. Also, these helped him develop a personal understanding of most of the circumstances and events that he is usually confronted with at any given period of time.

He does not forget to have some fun from time to time.

Essentially, he turns everything into a form of game where having some fun is considered as a kind of agenda. For this reason, he really enjoys mixing some work with pleasure. So far, he has successfully created a fun loving and an easy going culture in his work place.

Facing problems directly can help lead to a better future not only for yourself but also for the organizations and other things that involves you.

As soon as these personal and professional problems arise, he makes sure that he will tackle the concerns aggressively as soon as possible. In the long run, this ensured a better future for him and his establishments because these problems eventually did not turn out into worse ones because of negligence.

Branson makes every second count.

Richard Branson regards every moment that passes by as a form of opportunity for him to do everything in a better way. These moments can also serve as instances to help him improve a certain process in his undertakings or to perform the next few steps towards a larger objective. Usually, he makes every moment worthwhile by combining his business with pleasure.

He makes sure that he is usually open for changes in his personal life and career.

Being constantly open to possible changes in his approach, viewpoints, and perspectives to the concerns that he has to face made all the more an efficient and an effective person out of him in the long run. This is because the changes have eventually helped him attain both of his long term and his short term objectives and goals.

Branson makes sure that he meets new people along the way because they can serve as guides for him to establish a better professional and personal future.

He is a naturally passionate networker. Therefore, he really enjoys meeting some new people in the industry. More than meeting them, he enjoys building mutually rewarding relationships with them in the long run. He also finds pleasure in discussing new opportunities with them.

To help him get a better look at the future, he constantly steps out of his comfort zone.

He usually does for new types of industries that he has not thoroughly explored yet. Branson believes that when he faces the new challenges in these fields, he will be able to test his resolve, expertise, and discipline even more.

Looking for new opportunities is another good way to have a better view of the future.

He is constantly on the hunt for new ideas and chances that will make him have an advantage over the rest of his competitors.

In line with the previous points, he makes sure that he keeps on asking questions along the way.

Branson is regularly asks questions that highly focuses on solutions. These have since helped clarify his train of thoughts and aided him in overcoming his challenges that consistently flood him.

Challenging yourself constantly can help you get prepared for the future.

This is especially important because you are not entirely sure what the future holds for you. He considers everything as a goof chance to help him improve his expertise even more.

He is fond of trying new things.

Whether it be venturing in an unexpected or new type of industry or even flying some balloons over record breaking distances, it really appears that Branson will do almost anything at least once. This has helped him explore things that he never thought were there in the first place. This has introduced him to new ways to devise strategies for future use.

He makes sure that he always lives his life to the fullest.

He seeks out new and exciting experiences, adventures, and endeavors. Branson believes that his life should always be lived to the fullest potential.

His perspectives are considered as a vital tool for him to develop his deep sense of foresight not only for his personal life but also for his businesses.

It is somehow safe to say that he perceives his life differently than the multitude of people in the world. His type of perspective has ever since helped influence his emotions and driven his thoughts so he can experience things fully on a daily basis. The following are just some of his perspectives in life:

- He views money as a way to make things happen and not the end result in itself.

- He goes after his dreams. At the same time, he remains grounded in the real world.

- Branson clearly understands that he can always look for a solution no matter how large the problem seems to be.

- Richard Branson views life with that mentality that dictates him to work hard and to play hard.

Another thing that made it easier for him to look into the future is his current mindset.

Richard Branson has become successful in his craft because of the type of person that he has eventually become because of a fine combination of triumphs, setbacks, and experiences. These circumstances have eventually helped shape his mind in a lot of profound ways. In turn, these have enabled him to reach great feats that have gradually built his entire empire and fortune. His has then affected his future positively in ways that he never expected before. To help you unlock this type of mindset, you have to carefully examine his patterns of actions, language, decisions, and behaviors.

He makes sure that he has his main purpose set in his mind before he even starts off trying something.

The sheer act of creating a difference in the world where he dwells is considered as his primary purpose. This main purpose directs and guides all of his actions, behaviors, decisions, and choices.

As for his values, the sets them in a hierarchy that can help direct his daily decisions and choices.

The set of values that readily lie on top of the hierarchy highly influences his life and his ability to look into the future. His values have aided him to shape all of the circumstances in his life. While it may be difficult to specifically point out the hierarchy of the values, you may clearly identify those that will eventually mold his destiny. The following are just some of the set of values that help drive his decisions and actions:

- Competitions

- Contributions

- Teamwork

- Fun

- Frugality

- Adventure

- Entrepreneurialism

- Family

By progressively adjusting your personal set of values to it can closely match this list, you will discover that your actions, decisions, and choices will gradually start to match and align well with those of Richard Branson's.

Chapter 5 Philanthropic Work

"Ridiculous yachts and private planes and big limousines won't make people enjoy life more, and it sends out terrible messages to the people who work for them. It would be so much better if that money was spent in Africa - and it's about getting a balance." – Richard Branson

From being a record shop owner to becoming the head of the Virgin Empire, Richard Branson's focus is now on helping others out and saving the environment. Aside from entrepreneurship, Richard Branson also became known in activism. Branson delved into humanitarian initiatives as he strived to make a difference.

Richard Branson has had a lot of achievements under his belt: had ballooned across the Atlantic, had experienced floating down the Thames along with the Sex Pistols, and had been knighted by the Queen as well. He has become so successful that he even has his own island.

But if you think that this man is all about keeping his wealth to himself, think again.

What he had done is to pledge in committing $3 billion – all profits he has obtained from all his travel firms for the next 10 years – to help ease global warming.

Philanthropy History

"Student Valley Centre", the first charity started by Richard Branson, was built when he was only 17. This was a magazine all about youth culture, produced by students and for students.

He was also a patron of the International Rescue Corps, which is one of the few legitimate and independent search and rescue groups. This group is a charity registered in the UK that works solely on donations and operated completely by volunteers.

Come 2007, Richard Branson created The Elders.

The Elders Formation

In the later years of the 1990s, Branson, together with musician Peter Gabriel, went into discussions with Nelson Mandela about an idea of a small group of leaders whose purpose is to work objectively, setting aside personal interest, in order to solve significant global conflicts.

It was July 18th 2007 when Nelson Mandela announced the formation of The Elders in his speech for his 89th birthday in Johannesburg, South Africa. This group is composed of Kofi Annan serving as the chair, Gro Harlem Brundtland as deputy chair, Fernando Henrique Cardoso, Martti Ahtisaari, Lakhdar Brahimi, Ela Bhatt, Jimmy Carter, Graça Machel, Hina Jilani, Ernesto Zedillo, and Mary Robinson. Nelson Mandela and Desmond Tutu stand as honorary Elders. The funding of the group came from a group of donors which includes Branson and Gabriel.

Through their collective skills, The Elders attempt to push peaceful resolutions to age-old conflicts, devise new tactics for global issues that cause human suffering, and disseminate their wisdom by aiding the connection of voices all around the world. They deliberate carefully as to select the issues that they will prioritize.

Virgin Unite

In 2004, Virgin Unite was set up to make his staff get involved in worldwide social problems. Virgin Unite is also known as The Virgin Foundation that aims to combine entrepreneurial ideas with great people to make lives better.

Virgin Unite hatches new approaches toward leadership with groups such as *The Elders* (previously mentioned), *The B Team* and *Carbon War Room*.

a. The Elders – This is a group of independent leaders who work as one to exercise peace and human rights.
b. Carbon War Room – This is a group led by Jose Maria Figueres, a Costa Rican President, to assist in speeding and scaling solutions that deliver low-carbon economies. They also accelerate the capital flow and help remove market hindrances that prevent progress.
c. The B Team – Richard Branson coordinated with JochenZeitz, former PUMA CEO, to create a global initiative that aims to make business work for the

better. They are champions that go for making capitalism a great force for environmental, social and economic gain. They aim to shape a business future that's driven by planet, people and profit.

Virgin Unite also helps entrepreneurs worldwide as they start and grow their businesses, provide jobs and other opportunities. They also work with the Virgin Group to innovate people and help the planet even while gaining profits.

They all go for helping to create action that leads to a positive impact.

Other Charities and Causes

In 2008, Branson hosted a gathering at his private Caribbean island with Wikipedia founder Jimmy Wales, Former British leader and Prime Minister Tony Blair, and Google's Larry Page to discuss problems concerning global warming.

During Princess Diana's funeral, Richard Branson was able to convince Elton John to sing "Candle in the Wind", and this gesture soon raised $40 million given to charity.

He has supported more than 30 foundations and charities, and here are the more famous ones:

- Cancer Research UK, which is UK's leading charity that's meant for cancer research
- Greenpeace, an organization that focuses on threats to the planet and the environment
- Children with AIDS, a charity project set up in 1992 to assist children afflicted with AIDS and help them maintain a good life, and makes sure they grow up with neither prejudice or poverty
- Whatever It Takes, a one-of-a-kind artwork project that spreads hope by collecting artworks from leaders in fields such as music, film, sports, literature and royalty.
- Peace One Day, a group that aims to have an annual day without violence by working on education, documentary films and sports (football).
- Re*Generation, an initiative with Virgin Mobile USA and Virgin Unite that coordinates with partners to help the lives of homeless youth.

- The Eve Branson Foundation (his mother's charity), a group that aims to improve the lives of both young girls and women in the Atlas Mountains of Morocco through business, education and health care. They are given vocational training, educational opportunities, and other vital resources to make marketable goods and economic self-sufficiency.

Sharing the Fortune

It has been reported recently that Sir Richard will give half of his fortune to the needy. He, along with other billionaires has pledged to give half of their earned wealth hoping the act will make the world a better place.

Sir Richard has joined the *Giving Pledge* – an organization started by Bill Gates, his wife Melinda and Warren Buffett – and said they'll be using their money to create a peaceful world for people of the future to enjoy.

Richard Branson may be UK's fourth richest man, but he has this realization that "stuff" is not what really gives people happiness, but rather friends, family and good health. He's more than thankful that his children agree with him on this belief.

This realization came up during the early days of his marriage with Joan – they once lived on a houseboat, and it sank. They didn't miss anything except the photo albums. They experienced having their house on fire, and hit by lightning, and all they were concerned about is if everyone got out safely and without harm.

Sir Richard Branson will be using his wealth to assist more on social enterprises and for environmental causes. He sincerely believes that wealth should also work for the public good. These decisions that he made is not only an attempt to be remembered as philanthropists, but also a manner of protecting their children from the burden of having extreme wealth, which may eliminate them of any drive to achieve anything more in their own lives.

He aims to promote positive changes to become driving forces that lead to making the world a better place. He understands that he doesn't have all the answers yet and can't do it alone, that's why he works with other experts to have the information that makes lasting changes.

Branson School of Entrepreneurship

Branson has other works in South Africa. One is the establishment of the Branson School of Entrepreneurship that started in 2005. The school is set up as a partnership between Virgin Unite, Virgin's non-profit foundation, and TaddyBlecher, an entrepreneur who founded CIDA City Campus – a university located in Johannesburg. The Branson School of Entrepreneurship is established with the goal of improving economic growth in South Africa by aiding start-ups and micro-enterprises using mentors, networks, services, finance arrangements, and skills. To raise funds for the school, the Virgin group sponsored Sunday Times Fast Track 100. The annual event auctioned slots for joining Branson in trips to South Africa for coaching students are to attendees. In 2009, Practicus's Jason Luckhurst and Boyd Kershaw, Ainscough Group's Martin Ainscough, and Daisy Communications' Matthew Riley raised £150,000 through the auction.

Picnic Green Challenge

The first Picnic Green Challenge happened in 2007 where Richard Branson was the chairman of the jury. The challenge would reward €500,000 to the deemed best new green initiative. It was set up by "Postcode Loterij" (postcode lottery) from the Dutch and the PICNIC Network of Creative Professionals. Qurrent, with their QBox, won the challenge.

Other Efforts

Branson hosted a gathering in his private island attended by the big names in the business world, entertainment, and politics. In this gathering, they discussed about the problems the world faces because of global warming. They hoped that the gathering will be the first of many.

Richard Branson is one of the signatories of the Global Zero campaign – an international initiative that roots for the elimination of all nuclear weapons in the world. The campaign has garnered the support of over 300 leaders and 400,000 citizens.

Politics

Branson has been mentioned numerous times to be a candidate for Mayor of London. Polls among citizens made it apparent that he would surely be a strong candidate. However, he does not express any interest as of the moment.

Chapter 6: Attempts at World Records

"My general attitude to life is to enjoy every minute of every day. I never do anything with a feeling of, 'Oh God, I've got to do this today.'" – Richard Branson

Richard Branson, being a chaser of achievements, made numerous attempts of breaking world records.

In the spirit of Blue Riband, he tried to beat the record for the fastest crossing of the Atlantic Ocean. The first attempt of "Virgin Atlantic Challenger" was a failure. The boat capsized and he was rescued by RAF. Media coverage was rampant, with a number of newspapers calling for Branson to provide recompense for the government for the costs of his rescue.

Not fazed by failure as always, Branson went with a "Virgin Atlantic Challenger II" in 1986. With help from Daniel McCarthy, a sailing expert, he was able to snag the record – besting it by two hours.

Branson crossed the Atlantic a year later with a hot air balloon, the "Virgin Atlantic Flyer".

January of 1991, Branson broke another record as he crossed the Pacific. With Japan as the starting point, Branson flew to Arctic Canada in a hot air balloon. He reached speeds of up to 245 mph.

Branson, together with Steve Fossett and Per Lindstrand attempted to circumnavigate the world in a balloon. They broke a record in late 1998, being able to fly from Morocco to Hawaii; however, they were not able to finish a global flight.

Riding an amphibious vehicle, Branson also set a record in March of 2004 by traversing from Dover to Calais. It is the fastest English Channel crossing in such a vehicle finishing the trip in 1 hour, 40 minutes, and six seconds. 70 engineers created the Gibbs Aquada and it took seven years to finish. The amphibious vehicle can go more than 100 km/h on land and 30 km/h on water. Civilians can purchase the Aquada for $126,000.

In September of 2008, Richard Branson and his children failed at their attempt to set a world record for crossing the Atlantic Ocean via a sailboat. They endured strong winds and waves, as high as 40 feet for 2 days. They stopped the attempt when the strong current and waves wrecked their sailboat.

Richard Branson is known for not giving up. In 2012, he attempted to set two records, to be the oldest person to kite surf across the English Channel and to be the fastest to cross it. Along with his son, team and the media, they went to France to make the record happen.

Branson was able to kite-surf from Dymchurch, Kent to Wimereux, France in three hours and 45 minutes. This earns him the title, as the oldest person to have successfully crossed the English Channel while kite surfing. However, he was unsuccessful in his second goal, to be the fastest man to cross the Channel.

The fastest man to cross the English Channel was awarded to his son, Sam Branson. His son was able to kite-surf from Wimereux to Folkestone in just two hours and 18 minutes. Sam broke his own record in 1999, which was two hours and 30 minutes.

In the same year, LinkedIn awarded Richard Branson for having the most number of followers. He was recognized for being the first user to gain a million followers. He had 1,521,636 followers proving many people look up to him.

LinkedIn, a business-oriented social networking site aims to connect people from different industries. Employers can post vacancies in their companies, to find new talents and employees. While employees or individuals can use it to post career achievements and attract prospect employers, it's beneficial for small businesses, employees and the corporate industry.

The following year, Richard Branson set a new Guinness World Record for leading the most number of kite-surfers for one mile. Branson, together with his team of 318 people kite-surfed from Hayling Island under perfect weather conditions on September 15, 2013. Luck was on their side, as the weather was ideal for kite surfing allowing them to reach the one mile target.

In January 2014, Branson and his company reached another success. Its Virgin Galactic's SpaceShipTwo reached 71,000 ft during a test flight. They broke their record last September 2013 of 67,000 feet. This is a record high for the company indicating they are closer to launching their first space flight. Branson was quoted saying, "Today's flight was a success…progressively closer to our target of commercial flights in 2014".

If all works out as planned, Branson and his children, Holly and Sam will be the first passengers this Fall 2014 for Virgin Galactic's flight to space. This will be another world record for Branson and his company. He will be the first man on a commercial flight to space while his company will be the first commercial courier for space flights.

March 2014, Guinness awarded the title, "most people riding a kite surf board" to Richard Branson. What started as a dare from Branson's friend, Susi Mai led to a world record of having 4 people ride a surf kite. The challenge was held in Branson's private island in Neker Island, along with two other female and Susi Mai.

Branson known as an adrenaline junkie is thinking already of building a bigger board to see how many people he can accommodate while navigating the kite-surf board.

Recently, the Guinness World Record recognized Richard Branson as "the richest man presenter on a reality television show". This was in recognition for his 2004, reality show "The Rebel Billionaire: Branson's Quest for the Best". The show tested the capabilities of 16 individuals who can excel in the business industry. However, the tasks included performance of adrenaline stunts, which Branson is famous for. It was the only reality show that required contestants to travel to a new country each week. The show became #1 in countries like England, Philippines and China.

Richard Branson does not stop in setting and reaching for new world records. On his list is the Virgin Oceanic, a leisure undersea vessel that aims to dive in the five deepest oceans in the world within two years. Branson, together with Chris Welsh will make five dives in the following seas: Mariana Trench, Pacific Ocean; Puerto Rico Trench, Atlantic Ocean; Molloy Deep, Arctic Ocean; Diamantina Trench, Indian Ocean and South Sandwich Trench, Southern Ocean.

The Virgin Oceanic is set to make its maiden dive in the deepest place on earth, the Marina Trench. Solo pilot, Chris Welsh, will make the dive. If all goes well, Richard Branson is set to make the second dive near his hometown, the Puerto Rico Trench. Branson aims to set at least 30 world record from this project, and he also intends to help scientists and researchers explore and study the unreached parts of the ocean.

Aside from Branson's remarkable empire of achievements and wealth, he is also known for his passion for adventure and living life to the fullest. So, what are his reasons for continuously doing world record attempts? Below are his reasons:

√ Age doesn't matter

Richard started his entrepreneurial career when he was only 16 yrs old, by establishing the magazine, Student. At 22, he founded Virgin Records and from there, his empire grew. He ventured into different industries such as airline, food and more.

At 61, he still manages to do daredevil stunts and extreme sports, which only proves one is never too young to start nor too old to try something new.

√ Pioneer

His willingness to venture in industries beyond his comfort zone makes him a pioneer. Take for example the Virgin Galactic; it's the first commercial courier to take people into space. He always goes where no one would dare to.

Some of his ventures and record attempts may seem crazy for some, but for Branson, it's a learning experience.

√ Think Ahead

He always thinks in advance. He loves to innovate and improve things. He sees opportunities behind every problem. Like, during the time when fuel prices increased frequently, he decided to fund his own team to research on renewable fuel. He aims to offer green fuel and green solutions to the market.

√ Give Back

Branson does not only do extreme stunts and record attempts to gain fame. Instead, some of these served as fund-raising events to raise money for foundations. Also, in his latest project, the Virgin Oceanic, he aims to provide research materials for scientists to study on. He aims to work with researchers to expand their knowledge of the ocean, which may be used for the benefit of many.

√ Enjoy Life

Amidst his busy schedule and huge responsibilities, he serves as an example on how an individual must not forget to have fun. He incorporates his businesses into his hobbies. He funds sports teams while his company gets added exposure.

He's the perfect example on how a hard-working man balances his life with leisure and family.

√ Love what you do

Richard Branson makes it seems like managing an empire of businesses is easy. He's always full of passion and new ideas. Aside from his commitment to his companies, he is also emotionally invested in all the brands he owns.

You can also see that level of emotional investment in the stunt and world record he does. If he fails the first time, he doesn't easily get discouraged. Instead, he finds ways to improve his plan and methods.

Chapter 7 Lessons For Success

"If you're hurt, lick your wounds and get up again. If you've given it your absolute best, it's time to move forward." – Richard Branson

It is clear that Richard Branson lives by the code of not giving up when once, he was quoted, saying *"Fall down seven times, get up eight"*. Over the course of his life, starting from his academic endeavors as a child to the numerous personal and business controversies he's currently bothered with, he has endured a lot of trials. But even with knowledge of his limitations and a good deal of experience with failure, he came out undefeated. He came out strong in the end. Most people would just cower and give up when faced by the same tribulations that he struggled with. With it, they may just awaken many of the potentials they never even knew they had.

It's Not All about Diplomas

Is it a shocker that Richard Branson wasn't a hit back when he was in school? Well, it's true and mostly, it was due to the fact that he was dyslexic. He was diagnosed with a learning disability that stood in his way of making a mark in the academe. He found language subjects burdensome and he encountered a bit of trouble with math.

School may have taught him to understand and memorize but he hadn't quite enjoyed any of the lessons. After years of attending Scaitcliffe School and Stowe School in England, he dropped out. At 16, he officially called it quits and left the institutions empty-handed.

From all of his experiences with educational systems, he learned that success in life isn't heavily reliant on the recognition you've garnered from school. With what he has and who he is now, he knows that your fate in the present time is hardly dictated by anyone or anything else but you. He advises that unless you're willing to let yourself be impeded by the setbacks, you have to take on matters from here on out.

There's Freedom in Doing It for Free

Back when the name Virgin Records wasn't heard of, at all, Richard Branson was insistent of heading it with generosity. The very first man he signed in the 1970s was Mike Oldfield – a multi-instrumentalist. Clearly, the deal reveals that there was nothing for him in return. The musician hadn't quite promised him any reward but he couldn't care less. He wanted to be the owner of a record label, he says, and that how his business was going to be.

Though he wanted his record label to skyrocket to fame, he remained to be an advocate of amateur musicians. The first artist that used his studio wasn't instrumental to him in any way. From the man, he hadn't earned any cent and his business hadn't been promoted. For the passion in the industry that he's in, he supported him, which is a decision that he'll always be proud of himself for making.

Today, in his run with the record business, he hadn't just paved a name for himself; he also allowed artists who were never given a chance by others to let their work be heard. He wanted others to blossom, too, and he was willing to give them a hand.

Doing & Learning

Has it ever crossed your mind that Richard Branson, at his late 20s, went through with his first ever business venture with nary a clue about what he was doing? Indeed, it's no hearsay because when *Student* – a student publication - came to be in 1978, he just hoped it would be a success and did everything in his power to make that a reality.

In his opinion, excelling in a field is more about what you're willing to know than what you already know. His experience has introduced him to the truth that instances when dealing with the unknown is in your cards and they are inevitable. According to him, you're given the option to run from what's coming after you and you also have the option to man up and handle it. If you're anxious regarding what to do, don't panic. Virgin owner's take on it: you'll just learn as you go.

Be Fearless & Be a Starter

During the mid-2000s, Richard Branson went ahead and began his own space tourism company – Virgin Galactic. The objective of the business venture was privileging people to take sub-orbital vacations which would cost them an amount of around $200,000.

By far, it was an investment idea that was unusual. It was too dreamy, too risky, and not to mention the fact that it required a lot of money from people. However, in his opinion, there's a high chance of development for his space tourism company.

Regarding what he had done, he hadn't been short on making implications that often, it's mostly all about having guts. If you're unafraid to see new possibilities, he suggests, it's likely that you'll going nowhere but up.

Part of his success not just in the venture but in life, in general is his bravery. He used his frustration as fuel for creativity. He crossed lines that others never dared to. In the process, he didn't just make success for himself but caused changes in other aspects as well.

To others, he shares that probably nobody has trekked the same path you're planning to go on. But, you have to search for the courage to take the first step. As he would argue, daring to face uncertainties may be seemingly scary but sometimes the only escape isn't as promising. Sometimes, you have to scoot to where you think the gold is and sometimes, you will be right.

Revel in Simplicity

Richard Branson is a man who doesn't dwell too much on luxuries. Instead, he leads a simple life. Particularly, one that allows him the opportunity to value his loved ones and his health the most. As he was once caught saying, as long as his prized possessions are with him, he'll always be in a good place. Because of his down-to-earth personality, he can serve as the epitome of success.

He says that he isn't blind to the truth that his multi-billion life is worthy of envy. He insists, however, on proceeding with his daily agenda with mostly just the basics. For him, it's a great feeling that he has more than enough to get him by. But, according to him, when it all boils down to it, what matters more is the simplest of things. Thus, he has learned to prioritize his needs and has made sure that he's never put at risk.

On Giving

As of the early years of the 21st century, Richard Branson has established Global Zero (an organization that goes against the use of nuclear weapons), The Elders (an organization that strongly advocates against participation in wars), and Virgin Healthcare Foundation (an organization that is aimed at helping AIDS victims). He even signed up to back Al Gore financially on the American politician's fight against climate change. To all his different charities, he has contributed over $4 billion.

He presses that success isn't as valuable as it's supposed to be if it is not shared. He isn't the last one to admit that he's being preachy when saying this but he's familiar to the incomparable joy that is experienced once you have learned to impart what you have to others. After all, he believes, he owns a lot of money already and keeping it all to himself is no fun.

Don't Be Hesitant in Being a Star

In the late 1990s, Richard Branson released his autobiography called *Losing My Virginity.* He's aware that the title of his piece would draw crowds, which actually was what he was aiming for, and he hadn't let that chance go to waste. He knew that with that label, he could be a celebrated star and that was what happened.

As he would reiterate, humility is one thing; shying away from success is another. He shares that if you're the center of attention, go ahead and be it. Be dauntless in taking a ride to where the seemingly good things that belong to you are. The important aspect is, you still know your foundation and try not to let the higher essence have authority over you.

Just Be Happy

At his 60s, when most men in Richard Branson's age choose to simply stay put, he goes out there and gets his breath taken away whenever it can. Regularly, he kite-surfs, plays tennis, and swims lapses. He finds these pastimes relaxing. Apart from all these, he's not one to hold back from trying out his luck in breaking world records.

According to him, being triumphant in life doesn't mean anything if you're unsatisfied with where you are. He has days when stressors from his duties as a businessman but he believes that taking a break is good for the soul. He insists that the best way to be successful is to do what you love doing and be happy while you're at it.

Conclusion

Thank you again for downloading this book!

Finally, if you enjoyed this book, please take the time to share your thoughts and post a review on Amazon. It'd be greatly appreciated!

Thank you and good luck!

Lightning Source UK Ltd.
Milton Keynes UK
UKOW05f0448070617

302841UK00014B/536/P